Another 17 Prehistoric Beasts

EVERYONE SHOULD KNOW ABOUT

STANTON F. FINK

VOLUME III OF STANTON'S COLORING BOOKS

Acknowledgments

and Dedication

To my father, in whose books I discovered my first monsters.

To Will Caligan, whose help and encouragement is one of the primary reasons for this coloring book's existence.

To Mariano Silvera, who should have had his own artbooks

To Doctor David Morafka, who helped teach me to be more picky with my information.

To my friends, who helped push me to make this.

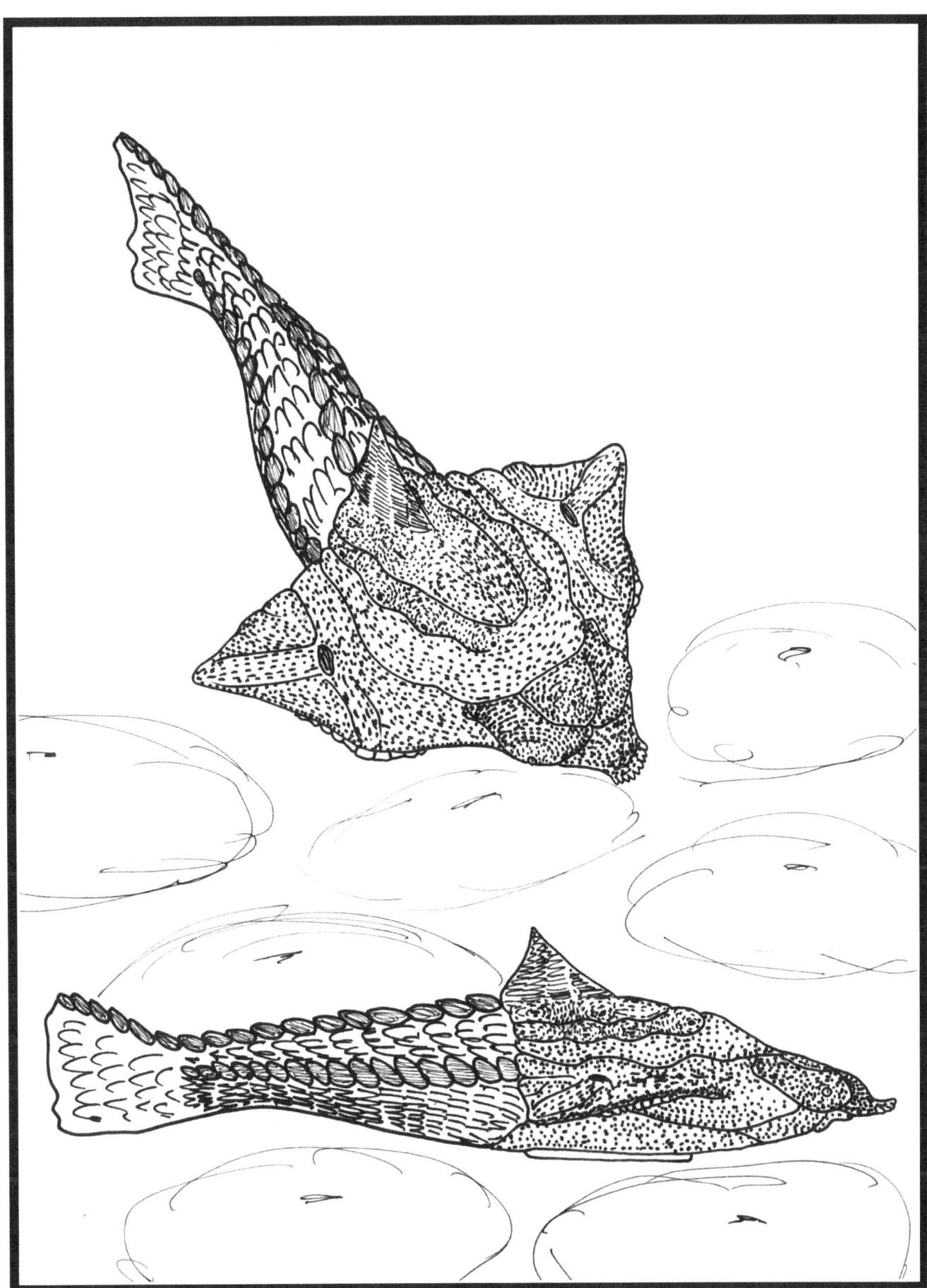

Table of Contents

Introduction

The purpose of this coloring book series is to provide information on various prehistoric animals both profoundly famous and incredibly obscure to artists of all ages. Of course, there is a lot of material to work with, as animals have been a major component of Earth's ecosystems for at least 670 million years.

For the sake of space and workability, each volume will contain 17 entries: ideally, one species for each geological time period, if possible. If you, or your inner and or outer child do not see your favorite prehistoric animal here, it may be eventually featured in another volume. Or, contact me to have it put into a later volume.

Glossary

- **Aquatic**- Living in water.
- **Arthropod**- Any member of the animal phylum Arthropoda, including trilobites, arachnids, crustaceans, insects, myriapods and their relatives. All arthropods have armor-like, jointed exoskeletons made of chitin-derived plates, sometimes reinforced with calcium carbonate, and jointed limbs.
- **Cambrian**- A period of time in the Paleozoic Era from 541 to 485 million years ago.
- **Carboniferous**- A period of time in the Paleozoic Era from 359 to 300 million years ago.
- **Cenozoic**- An era of time in the Phanerozoic Eon from 65 million years ago until now.
- **Chordate**- Any member of the animal phylum Chordata, including sea squirts, lancet fish, and vertebrates (such as lampreys, sharks, tuna, frogs, lizards, chickens, and people). All chordates have, at least at some point in their life cycle, a notochord, a long, flexible rod, usually made of cartilage, or, in the case of most vertebrates, cartilage and bone, running down the back from head to tail, directly beneath the neural tube.
- **Cnidarian**- Any member of the animal phylum Cnidaria, such as jellyfish, box jellies, Portuguese Man'o'war, sea anemones, coral and the parasitic myxozoans. Cnidarians are usually radially symmetrical, and have unique, venom-injecting stinging cells called "cnidocytes."
- **Cretaceous**- The last period of time in the Mesozoic Era, from 144 to 66 million years ago.
- **Devonian**- A period of time in the Paleozoic Era from 414 to 360 million years ago.
- **Ediacaran**- The last period of time in the Precambrian Eon from 635 to 542 million years ago.
- **Endemic**- The state of a species of organism being ecologically restricted to a specific location due to either having evolved there, or due to being that location being the last refuge of a former range. For example, the 'i'iwi honeycreeper, *Drepanis coccinea*, is endemic to the Hawaiian archipelago.
- **Eocene**- A period of time in the Cenozoic Era from 55 to 33 million years ago.
- **Fauna**- In an ecological context, "fauna" refers to the animal components of an ecosystem.
- **Formation**- In a geological or paleontological context, a formation is a group of rock layers.
- **Gnathostome**- A gnathostome is any vertebrate chordate with a moveable jaw (or had an ancestor with one).
- **Holocene**- A period of time in the Cenozoic Era from 12,000 years ago until now.
- ***Incertae sedis***- A Latin phrase literally meaning "uncertain seat." *"Incertae sedis"* is a term in classification used to refer to a species or group whose relationships with related organisms are unclear or poorly defined.

- **Jurassic**- The second period of time in the Mesozoic Era, from 199 to 145 million years ago.
- **Mesozoic**- An era of time in the Phanerozoic Eon from 249 to 66 million years ago.
- **Miocene**- A period of time in the Cenozoic Era from 23 to 5 million years ago.
- **Mollusk**- Any member of the animal phylum Mollusca, including snails, clams, squid, octopuses, tusk shells and chitons. Most mollusks have a calcium carbonate shell, and a toothed, file-like tongue called a radula. All mollusks have a cape-like organ, the mantle, which usually secretes the shell, and houses breathing organs, and a nervous system.
- **Nekton**- Any aquatic animal that lives either entirely or almost entirely in the water column, and relies on its own swimming or propulsion abilities to keep and move itself in and around the water column. Anchovies, porpoises and ichthyosaurs are examples of nekton.
- **Neogene**- The second third of the Cenozoic Era, comprising of the Miocene and the Pliocene periods.
- **Oligocene**- A period of time in the Cenozoic Era from 33 to 23 million years ago.
- **Ordovician**- A period of time in the Paleozoic Era from 484 to 440 million years ago.
- **Paleocene**- A period of time in the Cenozoic Era from 65 to 55 million years ago.
- **Paleogene**- The first third of the Cenozoic Era, comprising of the Paleocene, Eocene, and Oligocene.
- **Paleozoic**- An era of time in the Phanerozoic Eon from 249 to 66 million years ago.
- **Permian**- The last period of time in the Paleozoic Era, the time of "The Great Dying," or most severe of all known extinction events, from 299 to 250 million years ago.
- **Plankton**- An organism that uses water currents and waterflow to as its primary means of transportation in the water column because it is either too small to move long distances by its own power, or lacks the ability to propel itself entirely. Sargassum seaweed and jellyfish are two varieties of plankton.
- **Pleistocene**- A period of time in the Cenozoic Era from 3 million years ago until 12 thousand years ago.
- **Pliocene**- A period of time in the Cenozoic Era from 5 to 3 million years ago.
- **Quaternary**- The last third of the Cenozoic Era, comprising of the Pleistocene and the Holocene periods.
- **Rhopalium**- Singular form of "rhopalia." A rhopalium is a niche or a pocket along the margins of the bells of scyphozoan and cubozoan jellyfishes that house sensory organs, usually the eyespots and statoliths.
- **Sessile**- Living fixed in a single spot: sessile organisms include palm trees, adult barnacles, sea lilies, and garden eels.
- **Terrestrial**- Living on land.
- **Triassic**- The first period of time in the Mesozoic Era, from 249 to 200 million years ago.

Name	Burykh's Sea Squirt
Species	*Burykhia hunti*
Phylum	Chordata
Subphylum	Tunicata
Class	Ascidiacea
Family	Ausiidae
Size	Up to 135 mm high by up to 95 mm wide
Time Period	Late Ediacaran of the Precambrian, 555 million years ago
Location	Near Syuzma, on the Winter Coast of the White Sea, Russia
Comments	The Burykh's Sea Squirt, *Burykhia hunti*, named for a married couple who assisted the researchers who found the first fossils, is one of three chordates known from the Precambrian: of course, all three are identified as sea squirts. The fossils of Burykh's sea squirt suggest that the original animals were caught up in a violent landslide and were squashed flat. In life, the animals were very similar to modern-day, solitary sea squirts, in that they probably had free-living larvae which metamorphosed into sessile adults.

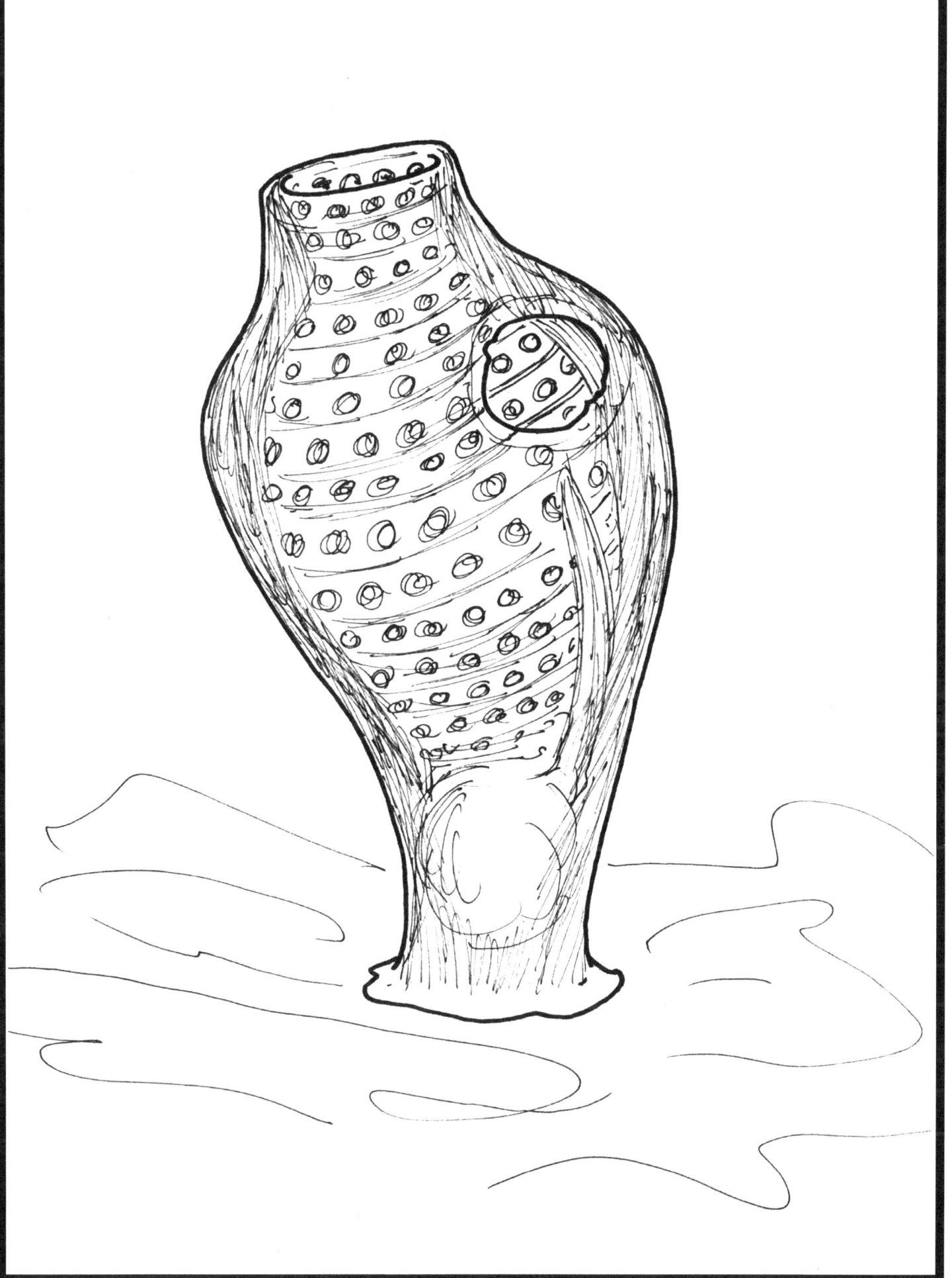

Name	Yunnan Sac-Jelly
Species	*Yunnanoascus haikouensis*
Phylum	Cnidaria
Subphylum	Medusazoa
Class	Scyphozoa
Family	*incertae sedis*
Size	Bell is 1 centimeter wide by 2 centimeters tall, tentacles about 1 centimeter in length.
Time Period	"Stage 3" of the Cambrian Period, 515 million years ago
Location	Heilinpu Formation, Kunming, Yunnan Province, China
Comments	When the first fossils of the Yunnan Sac-Jelly, *Yunnanoascus haikouensis*, was first discovered in 2007 as a member of the Chengjiang Fauna, it was originally described as a comb jelly. Recently, its fossils have been restudied, and now, the sac-jelly is determined to be a scyphozoan jellyfish, and is the earliest unambiguous example of a fossil jellyfish with sensory organs housed in rhopalia. What were originally thought to be the ctenidia rows of a comb jelly turned out to be rows of tentacles. In life, the Yunnan sac-jelly may have looked similarly to the much-larger, modern-day helmet jellyfish, *Periphylla periphylla*.

Name	# Cincinnati Sour Trilobite
Species	*Acidaspis cincinnatiensis*
Phylum	Arthropoda
Class	Trilobita
Order	Odontopleurida
Family	Odontopleuridae
Size	About 1 centimeter long
Time Period	Middle Ordovician, about 467 million years ago
Location	Near Cincinnati, Ohio, United States of America
Comments	The Cincinnati Sour Trilobite, *Acidaspis cincinnatiensis*, is a member of a long-lived genus of odontopleurid trilobites that ranged from the Middle Ordovician until the Middle Silurian period, when the last species' fossils disappear from the fossil record. Odontopleurid trilobites of the family Odontopleuridae are infamous for their extreme spinyness (or "spinosity"), especially in the Ordovician-aged genera. To humans' eyes, one would probably assume the primary function was for defense against predators, especially to discourage fish with big mouths. However, the sour trilobites of *Acidaspis*, and their relatives developed their spines before vertebrates developed jaws for suction-based predation. Other reasons for these long spines have been brainstormed, such as preventing the trilobites from sinking into soft mud. Of course, once jawed predatory vertebrates appeared by the early Silurian, the sour trilobites and other odontopleurids were well-prepared to fend them off. At least, until the middle Silurian, when the sour trilobites, themselves, disappear from the fossil record.

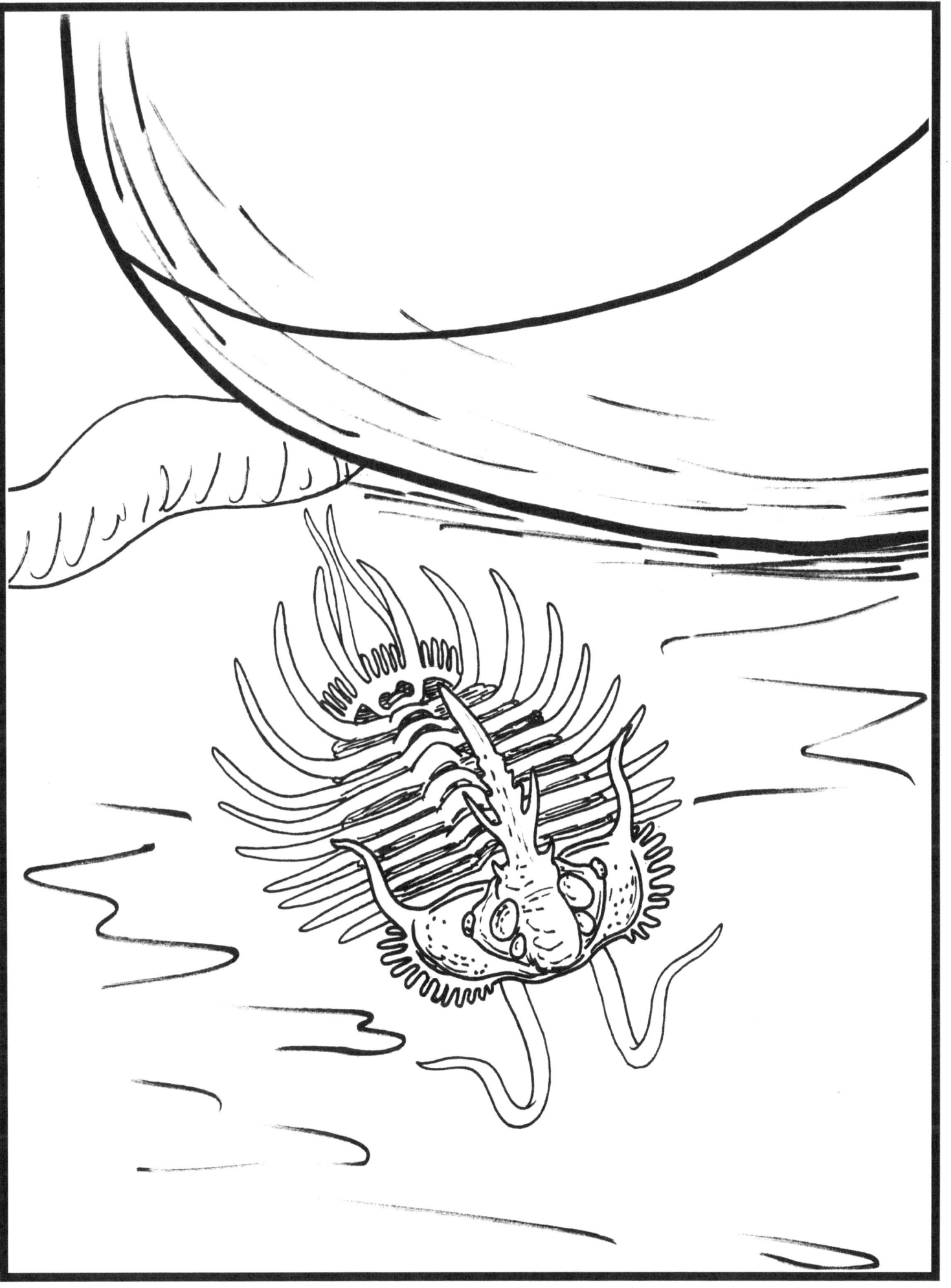

Name	**Warty Thyestes**
Species	*Thyestes verrucosus*
Phylum	Chordata
Class	Osteostraci
Order	Thyestiida
Family	Thyestiidae
Size	Living animal may have been up to 5 centimeters in length
Time Period	Ludlow epoch of the Middle Silurian, 423 to 421 million years ago
Location	Estonia and Sweden
Comments	The Warty Thyestes, *Thyestes verrucosus*, named for a mythical murderous Greek king, is a species of osteostracan jawless fish from shallow-water marine environments in what are today the islands of Saaremaa, Estonia, and Gotland, Sweden. The thyestes was originally thought to be a close relative of the Early Devonian osteostracan *Cephalaspis*. Recent reexaminations determined that the thyestes was not that closely related to *Cephalaspis*, and was, instead, more closely related to burrowing osteostracans like *Tremataspis*, which looked more like dinner rolls with scaly tails.
	In life, the warty thyestes probably swam close to the seafloor and rooted around in sand and mud, sucking up detritus and other edible particles from the sediment with its bellows-like mouth.

Name	Sand Pillow
Species	*Amphiaspis argo*
Phylum	Chordata
Class	Pteraspidiformes
Order	Cyathaspidiformes
Suborder	Amphiaspidiformes
Family	Amphiaspidae
Size	Armor about 24 centimeters long, live animal possibly 40 to 50 centimeters long.
Time Period	Early Emsian of the Early Devonian, about 407 to 405 million years ago.
Location	Taimyr Peninsula of Siberia.
Comments	The Sand Pillow, *Amphiaspis argo*, is an extinct cyathaspid heterostracan that lived in landlocked, briny lagoons that were cut off from the ocean during the Emsian epoch of the Early Devonian, in what is now Siberia.

Just before the start of the Emsian epoch, various cyathaspid fishes lived in lagoons in Siberia that were connected to the ocean; at the start of the Emsian, these lagoons were cut off from the ocean, and the cyathaspids living there evolved into the sand pillow, and its relatives, termed the "amphiaspids." The sand pillow and the amphiaspids differ from other cyathaspids in that all of the plates of the anterior armor were all fused together in a muffler-like structure. The sand pillow and other amphiaspids apparently had planktonic, free-swimming larvae that eventually developed into heavy armored, bottom-dwelling adults that buried themselves into the sediment up to their eyes or mouths, where they didn't do much beyond filter-feeding and leaving to find new resting places. The sand pillow and other amphiaspids went extinct soon after their lagoons reconnected with the ocean, allowing in jawed fishes that preyed on the defenseless larval forms.

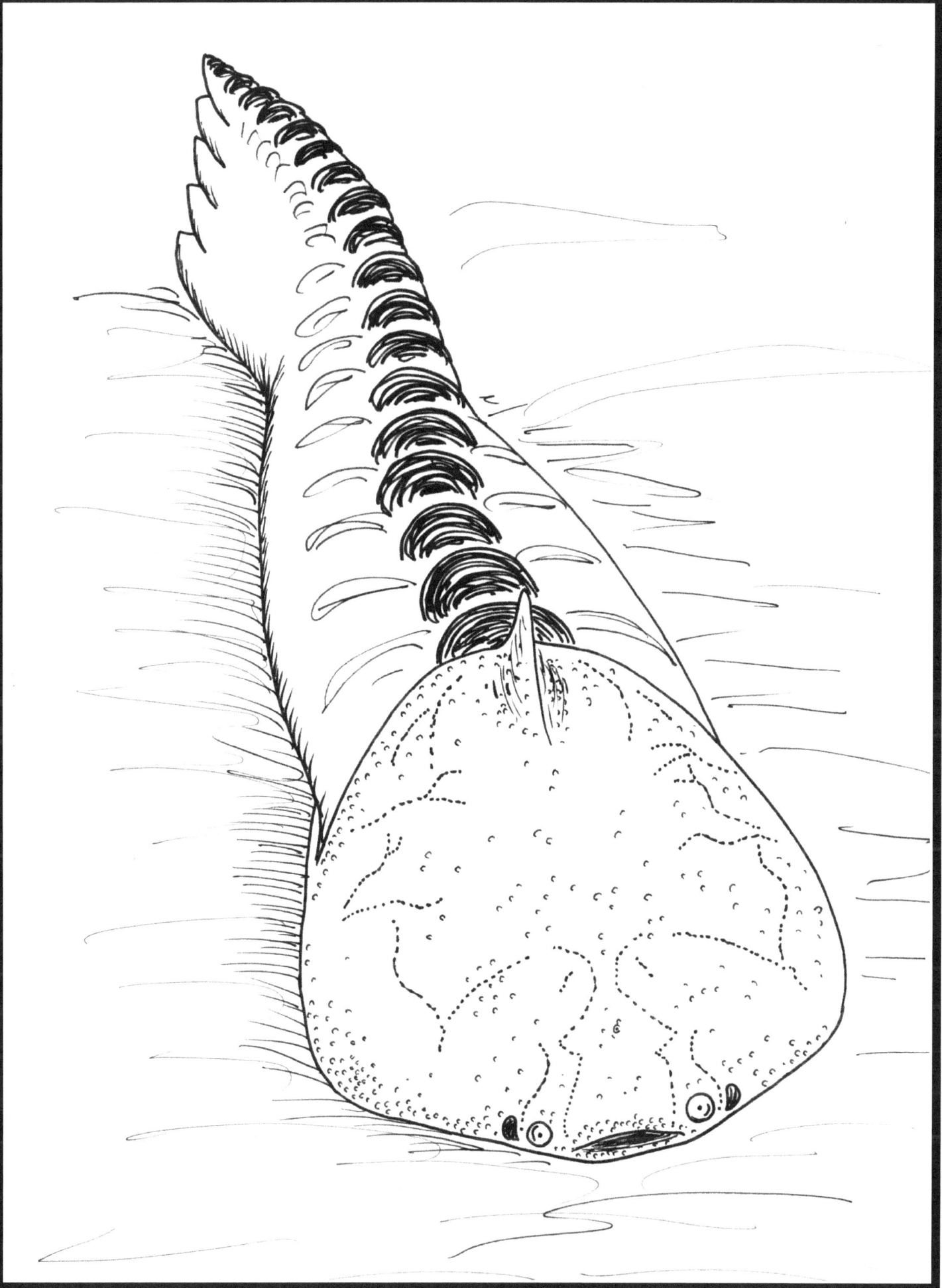

Name	Elongate Flamewyrm
Species	*Phlegethontia longissima*
Phylum	Chordata
clade	Reptilomorpha
clade	Lepospondyli
Order	Aistopoda
Family	Phlegethontiidae
Size	8 to 100 centimeters in length
Time Period	Middle Pennsylvanian epoch of the Carboniferous, about 300 million years ago
Location	Essex Biota of Mazon Creek, Grundy County, Illinois
Comments	The Elongated Flamewyrm, *Phlegothontia longissima*, is a legless, superficially snake-like lepospondyl amphibian from the Carboniferous United States of America (related species are known from early Permian Europe). The flamewyrms belong to a peculiar order, Aistopoda, which apparently represents the first group of tetrapod vertebrates to undergo the reduction of limbs. There is much speculation on the lifestyles of the aistopods, hypotheses of them being burrowers or swimmers, or leaf litter stalkers being very popular. Because all of the known aistopod skulls, many of which are light frameworks of bony struts, have long, needle-like teeth, all aistopods, the elongated flamewyrm included, are thought to be predators. Here, an elongated flamewyrm attacks a school of the temnospondyl tadpole, *Isodectes obtusus*.

Name   Proto Stem-Turtle

Species	*Eunotosaurus africanus*
Phylum	Chordata
Class	Reptilia
clade	Archosauria
clade	Pantestudines
Size	Maybe 30 centimeters from head to tail
Time Period	From the Late Capitanian epoch of the Middle Permian, about 266 to 251 million years ago
Location	Karoo Supergroup, South Africa

Comments

The Proto Stem-Turtle, *Eunotosaurus africanus*, is the most primitive "stem-turtle," or turtle-ancestor known, as the structure and articulation of its buttress-like ribs demonstrate the evolutionary foundation of the turtle shell. Similar ribs are seen in the Triassic-aged Turtle Grandfather, *Pappochelys*, of Germany, and the Chinese Toothed Bobsled, *Odontochelys*. The anatomy of the proto stem-turtle's skull strongly indicates the ancestors of turtles were archosauromorph reptiles, which included the ancestors of dinosaurs, crocodilians and pterosaurs.

The proto stem-turtle's fossils are among numerous animals found in the Karoo Supergroup formation in South Africa, which, during the Middle to Late Permian, was home to diverse ecosystems filled with reptiles, primitive archosauromorphs, and theraspids.

Name	Lotus Dragon
Species	*Lotosaurus adentus*
Phylum	Chordata
Class	Reptilia
clade	Archosauria
clade	Paracrocodylomorpha
clade	Poposauroidea
Family	Lotosauridae
Size	Estimated to be 1.5 to 2.5 meters long
Time Period	Anisian epoch of the Middle Triassic, about 245 to 237 million years ago
Location	*Lotosaurus* site of the Batung Formation, Hunan Province, China
Comments	The Lotus Dragon, *Lotosaurus adentus*, is a peculiar, beaked archosaur related to the superficially dinosaur-like shuvosaurids, the predatory rauisuchids and the crocodylomorphs (crocodilians and their immediate ancestors and in-laws).
	The toothless beak of the lotus dragon immediately brings to mind an herbivorous diet of shearing foliage and other plant matter. Enlarged vertebral spines, in turn, suggest a sail or an elongated hump along its back. The enlarged vertebral spines originally lead researchers to assume that the lotus dragon was a member of the Comb Lizard family of Ctenosauriscidae. Later analyses showed that the lotus dragon is actually most closely related to the bipedal shuvosaurids, and not the similar-looking comb lizards.
	The lotus dragon was a forest-dweller in what is now Hunan Province of China during the Middle Triassic.

Name	Inner Mongolian Orb Spider
Species	*Mongolarachne jurassica*
Phylum	Arthropoda
Class	Arachnida
Order	Araneae
Family	Mongolarachnidae
Size	Body length about 2.5 centimeters, leg span estimated to be 10 to 12 centimeters wide
Time Period	Callovian Epoch of the Middle Jurassic Period, 164 million years ago
Location	DaohugouBeds of Daohugou, Inner Mongolia, China
Comments	When the first fossil of the Inner Mongolian Orb Spider was found, it was assumed to have been an enormous male individual of a primitive golden orb spider of the genus *Nephila*, whose fossils previously only extended into the late Eocene of Colorado. When a second fossil of "Nephila" *jurassica* was discovered, this time of a female as large as the male, researchers immediately realized that this species of spider was not a golden orb spider, but was a species that represented a stage in orb spider evolution where the males had yet to become much much smaller than the female.
	Whether or not the Inner Mongolian Orb Spider, *Mongolarachne jurassica*, spun a web is not yet known. In the picture, a female is crawling down a branch of the gingko, *Yimaia capituliformis*, near the gingko-leaf mimicking scorpionfly, *Juracimbrophlebia ginkgofolia*, while a male Inner Mongolian orb spider is crawling up another branch.

Name	Freshwater Mosasaur
Species	*Pannoniasaurus inexpectatus*
Phylum	Chordata
Class	Reptilia
Order	Squamata
Family	Mosasauridae
Size	Estimated to be up to 6 meters long in life.
Time Period	Santonian epoch of the Late Cretaceous, about 86 to 84 million years ago
Location	Csehbánya Formation of Hungary
Comments	The mosasaurs are a family of extinct lizards that are famous for being marine predators of Late Cretaceous oceans. Thus, the finding of a mosasaur in freshwater strata of Late Cretaceous Hungary caught scientists off guard. Because most known reptilian, avian and mammalian animals that are obligately marine are, more or less waterproof, they can transition into freshwater environments provided they can find an environment with appropriate food and optimal temperatures.

The Freshwater Mosasaur, *Pannoniasaurus inexpectatus*, is a medium-sized mosasaur, and probably was descended from mosasaurs that followed fish up rivers and into a lake system that was in what is now Hungary. In this lake system, the freshwater mosasaur probably preyed on turtles, fish and amphibians, and competed with local crocodilians. In the picture, a freshwater mosasaur harasses an extinct sidenecked turtle of the species *Foxemys trabanti* in the hopes of having a lunch date with it.

Name	Turkmoonfish
Species	*Turkmene finitimus*
Phylum	Chordata
Class	Actinopterygii
Order	Lampriformes
Family	Turkmenidae
Size	About 11 centimeters long
Time Period	Late Thanetian Epoch of the Late Paleocene, 60 to 59 million years ago
Location	Danata Formation of Turkmenistan
Comments	The Turkmoonfish, *Turkmene finitimus*, is a very small extinct relative of the Opahs, *Lampris sp.* that lived in an offshore marine community in what is now the southern region of Turkmenistan, near the Turkmenistan-Iran border.

The Turkmoonfish, *Turkmene finitimus*, is a very small extinct relative of the Opahs, *Lampris sp.* that lived in an offshore marine community in what is now the southern region of Turkmenistan, near the Turkmenistan-Iran border.

This marine community had many different fish species, several of which were endemic, swimming crabs, and an endemic sea snake.

The turkmoonfish probably had a lifestyle similar to opahs or to the related sailfin moonfishes of the family Veliferidae; that is, a lifestyle of swimming about, sucking up smaller animals, especially small crustaceans.

Name	New Jersey Nautilus
Species	*Nautilus cookanum*
Phylum	Mollusca
Class	Cephalopoda
Order	Nautilida
Family	Nautilidae
Size	Adult shell about 10 centimeters in diameter
Time Period	Late Eocene, 41 to 38 million years ago
Location	American Eastern Seaboard, Oregon and Washington states of the United States of America
Comments	The New Jersey Nautilus, *Nautilus cookanum*, is a common nautilus that lived in what were once deepwater environments in what is now the United States of America, especially along the Atlantic Coast.

Much like modern-day nautiluses, the New Jersey nautilus slowly prowled about deepwater environments looking for shellfish and crustacean-molts to eat. Unlike modern-day nautiluses, the New Jersey nautilus, along with other Paleogene and Neogene *Nautilus* species, competed with nautilids of the genera *Eutrephoceras* and *Aturia* (with the Alabaman Aturnautilus, *A. alabamensis* pictured below the New Jersey nautilus).

The internal anatomy of the New Jersey nautilus' shell show that it represents a transitional form between nautiluses of *Nautilus*, and those of the genus *Eutrephoceras*.

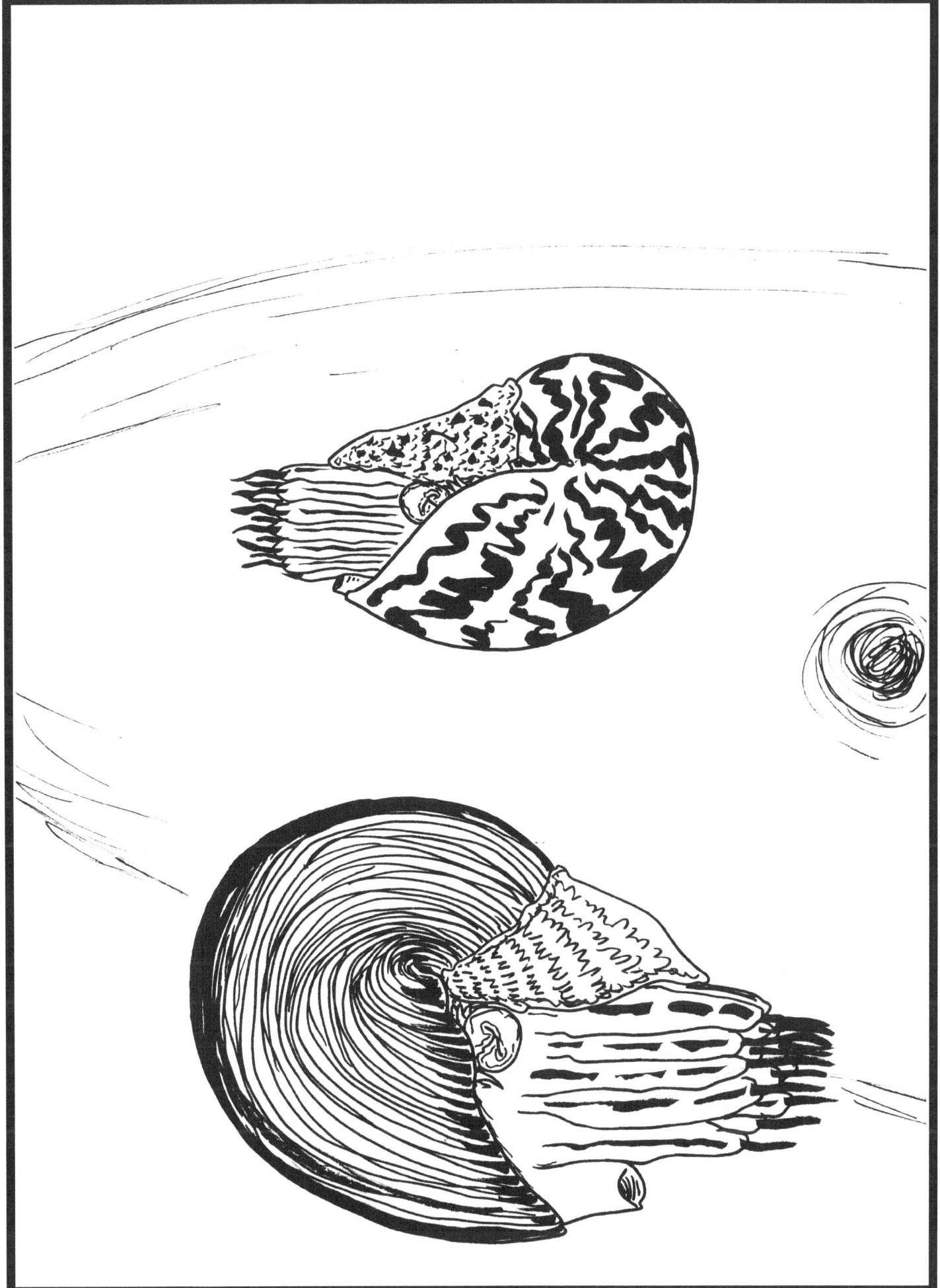

# Name	# Dwarf Basking Shark
Species	*Cetorhinus parvus*
Phylum	Chordata
Class	Chondrichthyes
Order	Lamniformes
Family	Cetorhinidae
Size	Maybe 2 to 3 meters long as adults
Time Period	Eocene until Middle Miocene, 50 to 10 million years ago
Location	Central Europe, including Germany, France, and Austria
Comments	

The Dwarf Basking Shark, *Cetorhinus parvus*, is the immediate ancestor of the Basking Shark, *C. maximus*. Most fossils of the dwarf basking shark are elements of the gillrakers, components of the gills that are used in filter-feeding, and which fall out upon the death of their owners, and are found in marine strata of Central Europe ranging from Eocene to Middle Miocene in age. An Oligocene-aged fossil of the back half of a juvenile confirms that the living animals were very similar, but much, much smaller than the modern species.

Because the earliest fossils of the modern basking shark date back to the Middle Miocene, the two species overlap temporally. However, no fossil sites are known that hold remains of both species, together, strongly suggesting that the two did not co-exist together.

Name

(Julia Anna) Gardner's Ecphora

Species	*Ecphora gardnerae*
Phylum	Mollusca
Class	Gastropoda
clade	Neogastropoda
Family	Muricidae
Size	Adult shell 4 to 5 centimeters
Time Period	Late Langhian to Serravallian epochs of the Middle Miocene, 15 to 12 million years ago
Location	Coastal Maryland and Virginia of the United States of America
Comments	Gardner's Ecphora, *Ecphora gardnerae*, named after American geologist, Julia Anna Gardner, is one of dozens of ecphora species, an extinct group of murex snails endemic to the Eastern Seaboard of North America from the Late Paleogene to the end of the Neogene. Ecphoras are descended from an Eocene murex, *Tritonopsis sp.*, and have no living descendants. The closest living relatives of ecphoras are the chorus shells of the genus *Forreria*, who are, ironically, endemic to the Pacific coast of California. The Gardner's ecphora lived in muddy and sandy bottoms off the coasts of what are now the states of Virginia and Maryland (and is Maryland's state fossil), where individuals sniffed out prey, primarily scallops of the extinct genus *Chesapecten*, and sometimes other, smaller ecphoras. Once suitable prey was found, the Gardner's ecphora would, much like most other murex snails, crawl on top of the victim, and use its radula to effectively lick a hole through the victim's shell. Once the hole has been made, the ecphora would extend its proboscis through the hole to gobble up the flesh of the prey at its leisure. Because some ecphoras were buried alive while in the process of feeding, scientists and fossil shell collectors know that ecphoras made distinctive, oval-shaped holes in the shells of their prey.

Name	Marsupial Sabertooth
Species	*Thylacosmilus atrox*
Phylum	Chordata
Class	Mammalia
clade	Metatheria
Order	Sparassodonta
Family	Thylacosmilidae
Size	Possibly as big as a modern jaguar, weighing up to 80 to 120 kilograms
Time Period	Late Miocene until the Piacenzian epoch of the Late Pliocene, from 11 to 2.5 million years ago
Location	Northern Argentina
Comments	The Marsupial Sabertooth, *Thylacosmilus atrox*, is a very large metatherian predator from a group of extinct, mostly carnivorous, South American mammals, Sparassodonta, which is closely related to marsupials. Whether or not sparassodonts nurtured their young in pouches like marsupials do is unknown.

The marsupial sabertooth preyed on other mammals, probably the various "South American ungulates," various endemic, herbivorous placental mammals. The skull of the marsupial sabertooth had a weak bite, and attachment sites for very powerful neck muscles: this suggests that the marsupial sabertooth subdued prey by seizing it and then stabbing it to death with its enormous upper canines.

Older texts often state that the marsupial sabertooth died out due to competition with the "superior placental" sabertoothed tigers of the genus *Smilodon* that entered South America during the Great Faunal Interchange of the Pleistocene. This is actually incorrect, as the marsupial sabertooth died out due to climate change at the end of the Pliocene, one million years before the earliest South American *Smilodon* fossils. Marsupial sabertooths more likely competed with other sparassodonts, indigenous crocodilians, and terror birds.

Name	Obscure Giant Deer
Species	*Praemegaceros obscurus*
Phylum	Chordata
Class	Mammalia
Order	Artiodactyla
Family	Cervidae
Size	Similar in size to a fallow deer
Time Period	Early to Middle Pleistocene, 2 to 1 million years ago
Location	Western Europe, especially common in Italy
Comments	The Obscure Giant Deer, *Praemegaceros obscurus*, is one of the earlier members of a lineage of mostly tremendous deer that culminates in the Giant Deer or "Irish Elk," *Megaloceros giganteus,* though, some species, such as the Cretan Dwarf Deer, *Candiacervus cretensis*, were as small as dogs.
	The obscure giant deer was a large deer similar in size to the related, still-living fallow deer, *Dama sp.*, but could be distinguished from fallow deer in that the second tine or point of the male obscure's antler was very long, and curving.
	The earliest fossils of the obscure giant deer are from Early Pleistocene sites in Italy: from Italy, the obscure spreads into Western Europe, where it is eventually replaced by other, later species of giant deer, such as the Vertical-Antlered and Dawkins' giant deer, *P. verticornis* and *P. dawkinsi*, respectively, during the Middle Pleistocene, whereupon the obscure giant deer then disappears from the fossil record.

Name	Elephant Bird
Species	*Aepyornis maximus*
Phylum	Chordata
Class	Aves
Superorder	Paleognathae
Order	Aepyornithiformes
Family	Aepyornithidae
Size	Up to 3 meters tall, estimated to weigh 400 kilograms
Time Period	Pleistocene to Late Holocene, from 2 million to maybe 1000CE
Location	Madagascar
Comments	The Elephant Bird, or Vorompatra, *Aepyornis maximus*, is the largest known avian theropod dinosaur known to humans, towering at a height of 3 meters, and had eggs as large as honeydew melons. In life, it probably looked like a gigantic, robustly built emu, though, DNA tests show that its closest living relatives are the kiwis of New Zealand. Because the elephant bird and all other modern ratites are flightless, it was once thought that their flightless ancestors were on the supercontinent of Gondwana before it broke up during the Cretaceous. However, with the discovery of Cenozoic-aged, flying ratites, as well as the DNA link between kiwis and elephant birds, it is now understood that the modern ratites' flying ancestors flew to where they are now.
	Hints of the elephant bird's life style are intermixed with fossils and Malagasy lore. The name "Vorompatra" means "bird (of the) marsh," suggesting that the animals lived in marshland, and that almost no bones show signs of butchering suggest there may have been a taboo, or *fady*, against killing the birds. The elephant bird's extinction was probably due to the destruction of Madagascar's forests and marshlands, a destruction that also claimed the Madagascan pygmy hippopotamus, *Choeropsis madagascarensis*, too.

Bibliography

- Antón, Mauricio (2013). <u>Sabertooth</u>. Bloomington, Indiana: Indiana University Press
- Croitor, R. (2006). "Taxonomy and systematics of large-sized deer of the genus *Praemegaceros* Portis, 1920 (Cervidae, Mammalia)". In Kahlke, R.D.; Maul, L.C.; Mazza, P.P.A. *Late Neogene and Quaternary Biodiversity and Evolution: Regional Developments and Interregional Correlations*. **1**. Stuttgart, Germany: Schweizerbart. pp. 91–116.
- Davis, Richard Arnold, and David L. Meyer. *A sea without fish: life in the Ordovician sea of the Cincinnati region*. Indiana University Press, 2009.
- Fedonkin, M. A., et al. "A new metazoan from the Vendian of the White Sea, Russia, with possible affinities to the ascidians." *Paleontological Journal* 46.1 (2012): 1-11.
- Frickhinger, Karl Albert *Fossilien Atlas Fische*, Mergus-Verlag, Melle, 1999
- Han, Jian, et al. "The earliest pelagic jellyfish with rhopalia from Cambrian Chengjiang Lagerstätte." *Palaeogeography, Palaeoclimatology, Palaeoecology* 449 (2016): 166-173.
- Hovestadt, Dirk C., and Maria Hovestadt-Euler. "A partial skeleton of Cetorhinus parvus Leriche, 1910 (Chondrichthyes, Cetorhinidae) from the Oligocene of Germany." *Paläontologische Zeitschrift* 86.1 (2012): 71-83.
- Makádi, L. S.; Caldwell, M. W.; Ősi, A. (2012). Butler, Richard J, ed. "The First Freshwater Mosasauroid (Upper Cretaceous, Hungary) and a New Clade of Basal Mosasauroids". *PLoS ONE*. **7** (12)
- Mitchell, K. J.; Llamas, B.; Soubrier, J.; Rawlence, N. J.; Worthy, T. H.; Wood, J.; Lee, M. S. Y.; Cooper, A. (2014-05-23). "Ancient DNA reveals elephant birds and kiwi are sister taxa and clarifies ratite bird evolution". *Science*. **344** (6186): 898–900
- Nesbitt, Sterling J. "The early evolution of archosaurs: relationships and the origin of major clades." (2011).
- Novitskaya, Larisse. Les amphiaspides (Heterostraci) du Devonien de la Siberie. Éditions du Centre national de la recherche scientifique, 1971.
- Rubidge, B. S., et al. "Eunotosaurus africanus from the Ecca-Beaufort contact in Northern Cape Province, South Africa-implications for Karoo basin development." *South African Journal of Science* 95.11/12 (1999): 553-554.
- Sansom, R. S. (2009). "Phylogeny, classification and character polarity of the Osteostraci (Vertebrata)". *Journal of Systematic Palaeontology*. **7**: 95–11.
- Selden, P. A.; Shih, C.K.; Ren, D. (2013). "A giant spider from the Jurassic of China reveals greater diversity of the orbicularian stem group". *Naturwissenschaften*. **100** (12): 1171–1181
- Squires, Richard L. "Cephalopods from the late Eocene Hoko River Formation, northwestern Washington." *Journal of Paleontology* 62.01 (1988): 76-82.
- Ward, L.W., 1993, Evolution of a name, or what species of Ecphora is that again? American Paleontologist, Paleontological Research Institution, Ithaca, NY, 1(2): 1-2.
- Wilson, D., 1987, Species of Ecphora in the Pungo River Formation, in C. E. Ray (ed.),

Geology and paleontology of the Lee Creek Mine, North Carolina, II: Smithsonian Contributions to Paleobiology, 61:21-29.

- Wittry, Jack. <u>The Mazon Creek Fossil Fauna.</u> Esconi, 2012.
- Wroe, S; Chamoli, U; Parr, WCH; Clausen, P; Ridgely, R (2013-06-26). "Comparative Biomechanical Modeling of Metatherian and Placental Saber-Tooths: A Different Kind of Bite for an Extreme Pouched Predator". *PLoS ONE*. **8** (6).
- Yoder, Anne D.; Nowak, Michael D. (2006). "Has Vicariance or Dispersal Been the Predominant Biogeographic Force in Madagascar? Only Time Will Tell". *Annual Review of Ecology, Evolution, and Systematics*. **37**: 405–431

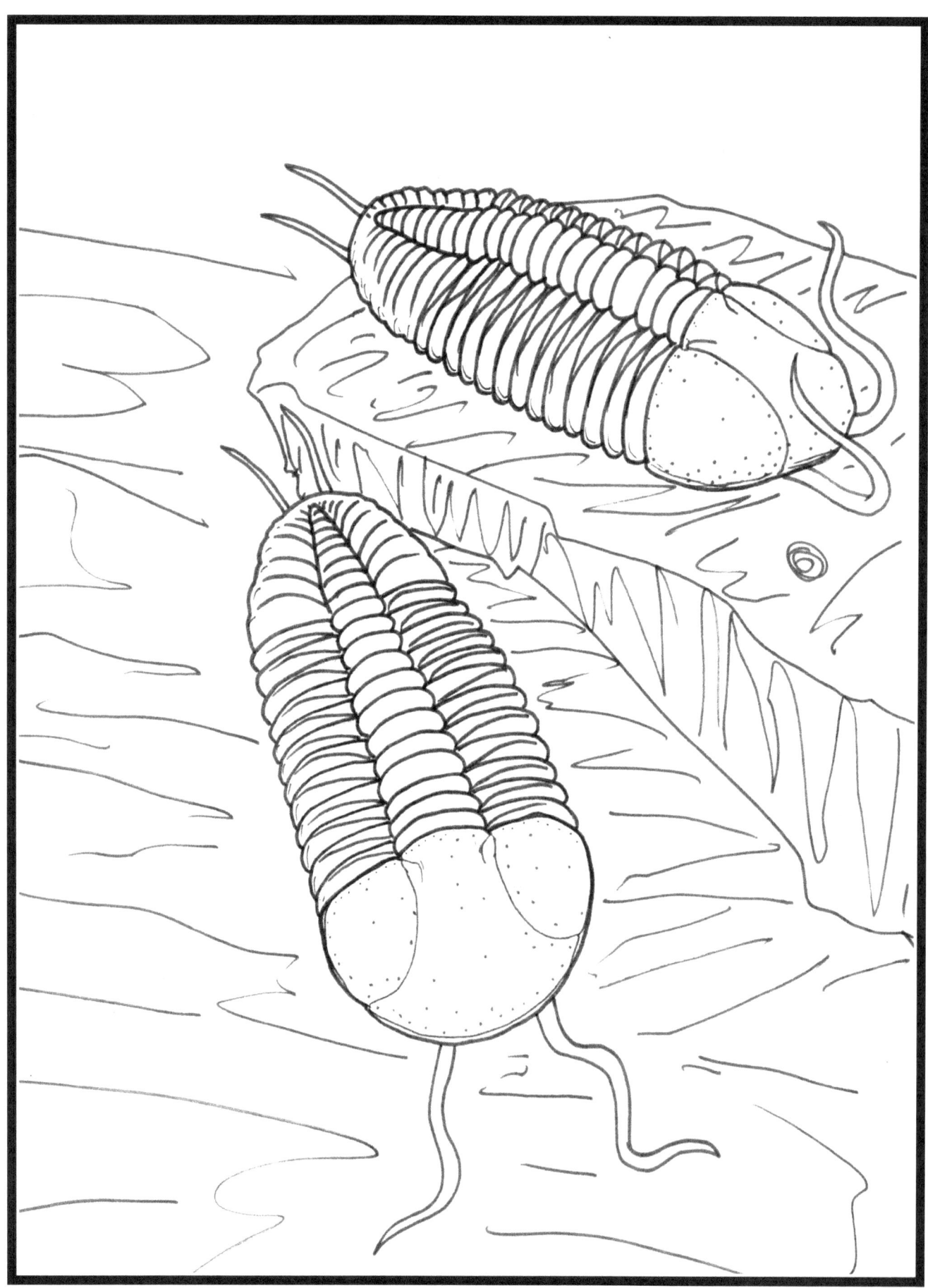

About the Artist

Stanton F. Fink is a student of Biology and Chinese Medicine, and makes a hobby of drawing monsters and researching flowers, arcane-looking creatures, prehistoric animals, fish, reptiles, birds and the occasional, really grotesque fungal fruiting body.

Stanton grew up and went to school in California and is currently living, drawing, and gardening in Oregon.

www.ingramcontent.com/pod-product-compliance
Lightning Source LLC
Chambersburg PA
CBHW081758280526
45789CB00008B/2904